The Chief Information Security
Officer (CISO) Handbook

Written by

Scott R. Ellis, CISSP, HCISPP, PCIP, CSO

Contents

About the Author

Scott R. Ellis, CISSP, HCISPP, PCIP has over 30 years in IT. He has held nearly every major position within IT having spent 10 years as an application programmer/developer, 10 years of networking (routing and switching) and 10 years IT Security. Mr. Ellis has served as a Chief Information Security Officer since 2011, and has focused heavily on the Healthcare Industry. He holds a Certified Information Systems Security Professional certification from ISC2.org, Healthcare Information Security and Privacy Professional certification from ISC2.org, and a Payment Card Industry Professional certification from PCI DSS Security Council. He studied business and management at Johns Hopkins University School of Continuing Studies, Baltimore, MD.

Introduction

This guide is designed to aide a Chief Information Security Officer (CISO) or the senior person in charge in building, maintaining, and augmenting a security program based on IT security industry standards and best practices.

The individual responsible will require significant knowledge of IT security best practices and standards, and ideally possess proper certifications, and have many years of IT experience to draw from.

This guide is designed to serve as a roadmap that can be used throughout the life-cycle of building, and maintaining a security program. It is designed to help you look at building a security program as a series of steps, but considers other dynamics like the role of education, and communications. It also looks at interpersonal relationships, and strategies to use to advance the security program based on the size or model in use of the security team.

This guide focuses on IT Security with an emphasis on the Healthcare industry, but notwithstanding healthcare specific regulations, is applicable in context to all industries. The steps are the same regardless of industry.

It looks specifically at the role of the CISO, and includes education and background requirements. It looks at the following:

- The CISO skillsets
- Building a Security Program from Scratch
- Security Organizational Models
- Communications and Executive Buy-in
- Executive Reporting

6

The Chief Information Security Officer

Background and Skillsets

This section takes a close look at the background needed to perform as a high functioning CISO.

The following represents the preferred minimum requirements:

- It is always preferable to have at least a B.S. in technology; but as typical of this industry, experience may be substituted for a degree.
- The years of hands-on and management experience within the IT security field should include a minimum of 10 years direct IT and/or IT security experience and at least 3 years' solid management experience.
- The preferred background is 10-15 years direct IT security experience and at least 7 years' solid management experience.

Certifications

There are many certifications that could be applicable to this role; however, the CISSP certification is really the most desirable. It's been dubbed the 'gold standard'. The Certified Information Systems Security Professional (CISSP) is the best option particularly if you only have one certification. Others may argue this, but it is a very comprehensive certification and it covers all the ground needed to perform as a high-functioning CISO.

In the case of Healthcare where HIPAA is a major regulatory requirement, the HCISPP is a great compliment. The HCISPP is Healthcare Information Security and Privacy Professional.

For those organizations that are handling customer or patient credit card data it would behoove you to consider at least a PCIP, Payment Card Industry Professional certification. One step more would be to consider becoming a QSA, Qualified Security Assessor within PCI DSS Security Council.

The CISO, Perceptions, Attitude, Behavior, and Demeanor

This section focuses on the person behind the role and gets into the details about what hard and soft skills are needed to perform as a high-functioning CISO and how they rank in the overall score. It looks at how the CISO is perceived, how your attitude impacts your success, how behavior and demeanor weigh in on your overall ability to communicate security goals and objectives, and obtain executive buy-in.

These are areas often overlooked but will determine whether you are successful and to the degree by which you are successful.

The 80/20 Rule

The concept of an 80/20 rule shows up in a lot of different venues. In the case of a CISO, and I will use CISO/CSO interchangeably from here out, the concept has to do with focus areas.

The 80- Knowledge and Expertise (Technical and Regulatory)

Eighty percent of what is needed to perform as a high-functioning CISO is knowledge and expertise. These skills will benefit you throughout your role as CISO. Here is a sampling of experience that you should have (you should score a minimum of 7/10 on each in terms of expertise):

- Email / Exchange / Linux / SMTP
- Network Routing and Switching
- Network Firewalls
- Intrusion Detection/Prevention Systems
- Network Threat Protection
- Advanced Malware Protection or Advanced Threat Protection (ATP)

- Endpoint Management (AV)
- Email SW to address spoofing, SPAM, and Malware
- Wireless networking and security (802.1x)
- Windows System Administration
- Virtual Machines, and virtual hosts
- Antivirus, Antimalware, BOTs, DDOS
- DHCP, DNS, SNMP
- Database Systems, SQLSVR, MYSQL
- TCP/IP (Packet Level)
- Physical Security (Cameras, Locking Mechanisms, Access procedures)
- Regulatory Knowledge (Healthcare, etc.)
  - HIPAA, HITECH, PCI DSS, HITRUST to name a few
- Standards and Best Practices
  - NIST/ISO
- Application programming experience (Java, PHP, HTML, scripting)
- Wireless Systems (WLANs, Routers)
- VPN and Remote Access in general
- Access Control and Identity Access Management

A good part of your day will be in making decisions about what is or is not a risk, evaluating technologies, SW, advising business units, and directing security priorities and implementations. If you do not possess the first-hand knowledge, you are going to have to go elsewhere routinely.

I am convinced you need to have a strong technical background to do this job right. This guide is designed to help someone that possesses the technical skills to plot out a course, establish a methodology, and build a road map to better protect any environment. Simply put, it's a tool.

The 20- Communications, Writing, Style, and Finesse

The other 20% of skills needed to perform as a high-functioning CISO are excellent writing skills, strong interpersonal and communication skills. This section considers attitude, demeanor, style, and finesse. These are what I call the soft skills. These skills are critical to success. They make up the smaller percentage in the 80/20 rule, but are equally necessary.

Workplace Perceptions & Demeanor

This is something that probably crosses your mind, but needs to be more deliberate. How others in the workplace perceive you is important from a team building, and team buy-in perspective. Do you come off as ill-tempered, emotional, defensive, or non-reactive, not easily flustered, calm, cool, and collected as the saying goes? It makes a difference, a big difference.

This section gets into the psychology of interpersonal communications. These things I have learned over the course of 30 years in IT. I invite you to draw your own conclusions.

Perceptions

There are not a lot of things you can control, but I maintain your attitude is one of them. Here is a simple strategy that I have heard quoted, "don't react, act". Taking this position can save you a lot of difficulty with peers and senior executives. Try to get into the habit of not responding out of emotion. Step off the plate, think about what you are trying to achieve and what communication strategy will help you get there. Communication must always serve a purpose either deliberately or not. Make it deliberate. Take the high road, be smart. Strong leaders are confident and poised.

Appearance and Language

Let's talk about your demeanor. Dress matters. Communication style matters. Behavior matters. You can never go wrong by dressing right. Always try to match or exceed the dress code. If it is casual, make it business casual. Set the bar.

What about communication style? Do you use inappropriate words to express yourself? I maintain in business; you should never do that. People judge you for it, even if they do it. Be well spoken, with manners; be kind and courteous, especially to subordinates. Treat those that report to you as you are serving them. Don't take them for granted. Many people do.

Body language is often more of a topic today than ever before. Do you have any habits that people could find offensive? I am serious. People are always judging you. I am not going to spell them out, just think about it. Is there anything I do, that someone could call me out on?

How to Interface with Peers, Subordinates, and Executives

Peers

Interfacing with peers can be challenging, especially when they report to someone different than you. When your peers report to the same manager, he or she can sort out things. They can address issues and are a source of escalation when the time comes.

Working with peers requires you to be extremely attentive to details. You must understand what they are trying to do with their team and individually. You need to understand what areas will pose a struggle or not.

In security, you often have to work in an environment such as this. You need cooperation. So, develop the relationships. Put forth the energy to work well together. This does not mean you do not hold a strong position, it just means you are investing in the individual and gaining their respect.

The bottom-line is that security professionals need as many people as possible to support the mission and treat it with a sense of priority. You've heard the saying, 'security is everyone's responsibility'. Gain the respect of your peers, and find ways to help them solve some of their problems; get them on board with your security program.

Subordinates

Working with people that report to you takes a special kind of focus. Your goal is to find their individual strengths, and align them with the security work to be done. This is no different than coaching a team, you should know what each one brings to the table, and then position them accordingly.

Once you have identified their individual strengths, play to them. This will give them confidence and satisfaction in their work. Find ways to motivate them to do more. There always seems to be a shortage of security team members. There is always more work to be done then there are resources to do it.

A strong leader knows this and uses this knowledge to maximize productivity and results.

Executives

The executives require a lot of communication, and education is usually a big part of that communication. They need to understand investments into security technology and tools, restrictions on behavior, and infringes on their own productivity balancing security with efficiency and business mission.

You need to align security with business mission, goals and objectives in a way that advances both. It's my position that you should always be able to advance security in a way that does not take away from the business. Improving the business and its profitability is still job one.

Approach security as a business function with executives and you will be well on your way to obtaining needed buy-in from them along the way. Look for ways to demonstrate how investing in certain security technologies will reduce risks, and save money by reducing the likelihood of a breach of data. Use tools like Single Loss Expectancy (SLE) and Annual Loss Expectancy (ALE) to outline the risk avoidance value proposition.

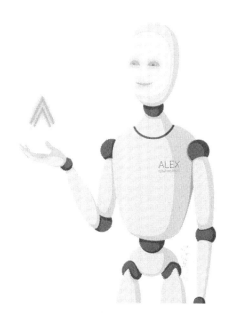

ALE

is an acronym for

Annual Loss Expectancy

⏻

by allacronyms.com

Here is an example of ALE:

Single Loss Expectancy $100 year.

Exposure rate is 30%.

Annualized Frequency .5.

Annual Loss Expectancy is $15.

Obviously, this is a very small scale, but suitable for an example. You will be working with 1000's of dollars. There are calculators on the internet that will perform the calculation for you, but in reviewing this example, it should be clear how the formula works.

With ALE of $15, you would not want to spend more than that to mitigate it.

Building an Enterprise Security Program from Scratch

The concept of building a security program in the absence of one is daunting. If you do not have a comprehensive background in IT security and have never done this, I am going to provide you with an outline that you can use. I am going to lay out a complete roadmap that anyone can follow.

The Building Blocks

The building blocks that make up any security program consist of the following

- Risk Assessments (HIPAA, NIST, ISO, PCI DSS)
- Vulnerability Scans & Penetration Testing; Annual Audits
- Plan of Action and Milestones
- Security Plan (Tactical and Strategic)
- Security Policy Development
- Security Procedures
- Security Budget
- Security Training and Awareness
- Quarterly Security Reviews
- Annual Refresh

Risk Assessments

I am going to layout sources that you can use to develop your risk assessment, but before doing so, I want to make clear what you are trying to do. The goal of the risk assessment is to identify where your risks are. As part of the risk assessment, you need to identify where your critical assets are. You need to know where the sensitive data resides that you have an obligation to protect. By sensitive data, I am talking about Personally Identifiable Information (PII), Protected Healthcare Information (PHI), and credit card data (PCI DSS). Furthermore, if you do not know what sensitive data you have and where, how can you build a strategy to protect it? Please keep this concept in mind throughout this guide.

HIPAA

Performing a risk assessment is fundamental. In the case of Healthcare, you must perform a HIPAA risk assessment based on the HIPAA security rule. You can learn more about the HIPAA security and privacy rule at the following location: http://www.hhs.gov/hipaa/for-professionals/security/index.html

NIST

However, HIPAA is not comprehensive enough, so it is recommended that you consider a (NIST) National Institute of Standards and Technology based risk assessment using the Special Publications (SP) 800 series guides. Performing a NIST based risk assessment means using one of the most comprehensive standards available.

Please review the NIST publications and the SP 800-53.
http://csrc.nist.gov/publications/PubsSPs.html

PCI DSS

If you perform credit card processing, then you need to understand PCI DSS. There are very specific requirements that must be adhered to or you risk fines and penalties. Largely speaking HIPAA and PCI DSS requirements roll up into the NIST requirements, which is what I consider the gold standard for IT Security.

Additional information can be found at this location: https://www.pcisecuritystandards.org/

Plan of Action & Milestones

The Plan of Action is based on a review of the mid-level and high-level risks identified as part of the Risk Assessment.

One theme that will resound is the concept of prioritization. In my opinion, there is always an inherent priority to IT security. This is particularly important, because there is also typically a lack of resources to be had, and most often capital.

Whether you have performed a HIPAA, NIST/ISO, or PCI DSS risk assessment, you need to focus on the priority mid-level and high-level risks identified. You can always circle back to the low-level items, but try and get a handle on the priority risks first.

The Plan of Action should include a list of all the mid-level and high-level risks identified, the reference number to the source risk assessment, mitigation strategy, budgetary requirements, and timelines with proper identification of milestones required to demonstrate mitigation is complete. In many cases, this is referred to as a Gap Assessment.

Risk	Risk # (ref)	Mitigation	Priority	Milestone1	Milestone2	Capital?

Security Prioritization

This section focuses on a methodology for assigning priority to security activities. Everything in security has an ultimate priority based on the changing cyber threat landscape. The threat landscape is fluid and priorities shift. As the focus of threat actor's change, so must yours. Therefore, this methodology considers how often priorities should change to align with the changing cyber threat landscape.

The end-game here is a methodology for assigning security priority that is re-evaluated periodically. It has the following characteristics:

1. Criteria set for assigning security priority.
2. Frequency that security priority is re-evaluated.
3. Assignment of security priority.

All IT security organizations should develop a tactical and strategic plan. There is a charter, road map, and action plans. There are also security priorities. This section will help in determining ultimate priority for all of the security activities in play, and provide a mechanism for analyzing future trends.

Defining Security Priority

The best way to determine security priority is by understanding the historical context as well as current, and projected (trending) threat landscape. The historical threat landscape includes the last 12 – 18 months of threat analysis. It could be stated that current is equal to a calendar time period (up to 12 months in a calendar year).

Since most security analysis is done on a yearly basis, it is reasonable to conclude that the current period includes the current year.

The projected or trending threat landscape is part of an aggregate study where trends are identified and the likelihood of increase or decrease is somewhat predictable. The projected threat landscape could go forward but not more than 12 – 18 months, in my opinion.

Regardless of methodology, your tactical response should be able to adapt quickly to a new or unknown threat. Leave room for the unexpected.

In order to effectively determine security priority, it is recommended that some elements be weighted to ensure proper priority in the overall context.

In the case of HIPAA and PCI, it is recommended that the security priority weight be set to HIGH. Even without a security incident that results in a data breach, there are penalties and fines for non-compliance.

Healthcare and HIPAA (Weight is set to HIGH)

The Healthcare industry has its own set of requirements. Healthcare is under the regulatory control of the federal government, Health and Human Services ('HHS') and HIPAA.

This adds a layer of complexity in the sense that there are fines and penalties for non-compliance. The states' also have their own criteria for data that is breached and have specific reporting requirements, actions, and time frames.

Therefore, HIPAA (Security Rule) requirements must be considered in the overall prioritization schema.

Below is a synopsis of the HIPAA security rule requirements taken from the final security rule from "HHS HIPAA Security Rule Final 2003 Version":

Appendix A to Subpart C of Part 164—Security Standards: Matrix
Standards Sections Implementation Specifications (R)=Required, (A)=Addressable

Administrative
Security Management Process................. 164.308(a)(1) Risk Analysis (R)
Risk Management (R)
Sanction Policy (R)
Information System Activity Review (R)
Assigned Security Responsibility................ 164.308(a)(2) (R)
Workforce Security .... 164.308(a)(3) Authorization and/or Supervision (A)
Workforce Clearance Procedure
Termination Procedures (A)
Information Access Management .... 164.308(a)(4) Isolating Healthcare Clearinghouse Function (R)
Access Authorization (A)
Access Establishment and Modification (A)
Security Awareness and Training .... 164.308(a)(5) Security Reminders (A)
Protection from Malicious Software (A)
Log-in Monitoring (A)
Password Management (A)
Security Incident Procedures................... 164.308(a)(6) Response and Reporting (R)
Contingency Plan....................................... 164.308(a)(7) Data Backup Plan (R)
Disaster Recovery Plan (R)
Emergency Mode Operation Plan (R)
Testing and Revision Procedure (A)
Applications and Data Criticality Analysis (A)
Evaluation .... 164.308(a)(8) (R)
Business Associate Contracts and Other Arrangement.
164.308(b)(1) Written Contract or Other Arrangement (R)
Physical Safeguards
Facility Access Controls .... 164.310(a)(1) Contingency Operations (A)
Facility Security Plan (A)

Copyright Scott R. Ellis © 2016 All Rights Reserved

Access Control and Validation Procedures (A)
Maintenance Records (A)
Workstation Use .... 164.310(b) (R)
Workstation Security .... 164.310(c) (R)
Device and Media Controls .... 164.310(d)(1) Disposal (R)
Media Re-use (R)
Accountability (A)
Data Backup and Storage (A)
Technical Safeguards (see § 164.312)
Access Control .... 164.312(a)(1) Unique User Identification (R)
Emergency Access Procedure (R)
Automatic Logoff (A)
Encryption and Decryption (A)
Audit Controls .... 164.312(b) (R)
Integrity.. 164.312(c)(1) Mechanism to Authenticate Electronic Protected Health Information (A)
Person or Entity Authentication ....164.312(d) (R)
Transmission Security .... 164.312(e)(1) Integrity Controls (A)
Encryption (A)

PCI (Weight is set to HIGH)

Payment Card Industry ('PCI') has its own set of requirements for those businesses that process payments using credit cards. Customer card-holder data must be protected, and there are significant requirements associated with protecting the sensitive card-holder data.

Below is a summary list from the PCI DSS Security Council website.

Basic Requirements of PCI DSS

The PCI Data Security Standard consists of 12 requirements that have been laid down fewer than 6 different categories.

Objectives	PCI DSS Requirements
Build and Maintain a Secure Network and Systems	1. Install and maintain a firewall configuration to protect cardholder data
	2. Do not use vendor-supplied defaults for system passwords and other security parameters
Protect Cardholder Data	3. Protect stored cardholder data
	4. Encrypt transmission of cardholder data across open, public networks
Maintain a Vulnerability Management Program	5. Protect all systems against malware and regularly update anti-virus software or programs
	6. Develop and maintain secure systems and applications
Implement Strong Access Control Measures	7. Restrict access to cardholder data by business need to know
	8. Identify and authenticate access to system components
	9. Restrict physical access to cardholder data
Regularly monitor and test networks	10. Track and monitor all access to network resources and cardholder data
	11. Regularly test security systems and processes.
Maintain an Information Security Policy Maintain a policy that addresses information security	12. Maintain a policy that addresses information security for all personnel

for all personnel.

National Institute of Standards & Technology ('NIST')

The NIST special publications for information security are very comprehensive and roll up the requirements of both HIPAA and PCI. Using NIST you have the advantage of ensuring that both HIPAA and PCIs' regulatory requirements are met.

Historical View

When it comes to establishing a historical context, it helps to have sources. By sources, I am talking about annual reports that focus on the cyber threat landscape and aggregate data.

One of the reports that I have used for many years is Verizon's Data Breach Investigative Report ('DBIR'). For many years, Verizon has done extensive reporting.

The 2015 report can be obtained from the following link:

www.verizonenterprise.com/**DBIR**/2015

The Ponemon Institute and SANs also provide annual reports. There are many to choose from, but Verizon's is extremely comprehensive and looks at security across all major industries.

Current View

The context for the current view of the Cyber Threat Landscape includes the following attributes:

- News Reporting (TV and Late Breaking News)
- The Internet – IT Security Forums and Websites
- National Security Advisories (FBI, DHS)
- Industry Groups

Cyber security has become a huge topic in the media due to the proliferation of cyber-attacks. Cyber threat activity is at an all-time high. We are faced with cyber-attacks daily, and not every incident makes the news.

The cyber threat continues to increase year after year with no end in sight. <u>This means that cyber security needs to be one of the highest focus areas of any modern-day business</u>. A business strategic plan that does not consider cyber security is not in touch. Many businesses have begun to evolve the role of the CISO/CSO to report directly to the CEO.

Forward Looking View

Trying to get a fix on where the next attack is coming from is not easy. However, there are markers. This is where trending comes into play. There are many sources that document patterns over time that seek to diagnose and to some degree predict with reasonable accuracy areas of threat that will likely continue or be on the rise. In some cases, identify threat vectors that are on the decrease too.

Criteria

When determining priority, I use the following:

- Immediate threats
- Weighted priority (regulatory requirements)
- Cyber-threat historical and current contexts
- Industry specific threat vectors and forward looking views

Immediate threats require immediate action and for this reason supersede all other priorities. Immediate threats are always <u>tactical</u> in nature.

Weighted priority should be slated at the top of the overall list, because in the absence of a security incident there may be fines and penalties due to non-compliance.

However, weighted priority should be considered in the overall context of known security risks within an organization.

Cyber-threats historical and current year contexts are most applicable as they underline which risks are likely to be taken advantage of.

Industry specific threat vectors allow you to drill down another layer to hone in on the likelihood of an attack.

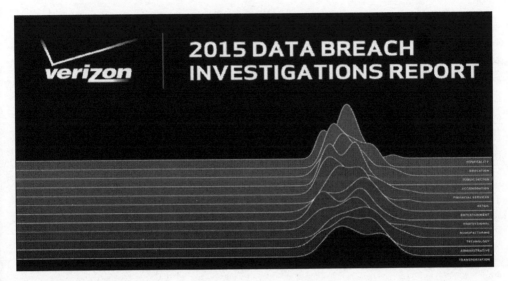

Verizon's DBIR 2015 Report

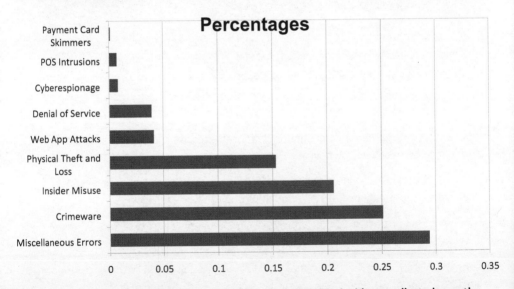

"The headliner from the 2014 DBIR was that 92% of all 100,000+ incidents collected over the last 10 years fell into nine basic patterns. Thankfully, that finding held true this past year as well (96%), so we avoid getting egg on our face. Frequency of incident classification patterns across security incidents while the threats against us may "seem" innumerable, infinitely varied, and ever-changing, <u>the reality is they aren't</u>." Verizon DBIR 2015 report.

Security Sources - Healthcare

In reviewing industry-specific data within the health-care industry, it is possible to see the overall cohesion that exists in comparison to the aggregate data across all industries. The patterns align with overall industry threat vectors.

The following chart is taken from Verizon's Protected Health Information Data Breach Report for 2015.

In comparing both charts, Physical, Error, and Misuse represent the largest overall threat vector.

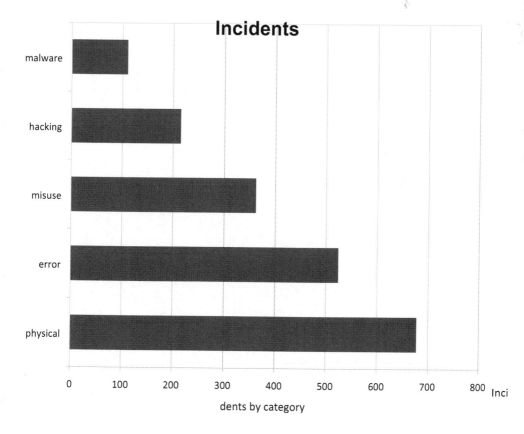

Assigning Security Priority

Based on the overall industry threat data, and the health-care DBIR data, physical theft and loss, miscellaneous employee errors, and insider misuse represent the lion's share of threats / risks to be mitigated.

Security Prioritization -Putting it all together

So, what does all this mean? How do I apply this data in a way that considers various security priorities?

All the various threat vectors or risks have a mitigation counterpart. Here is how I see it.

IT security and industry specific data:

- Theft and Loss (The most significant threat vector within HealthCare) Front-line Defenses:

  - Encryption

  - Two-Factor Authentication

  - Password Management / Access Controls

  - Device Management (MDM)

- Miscellaneous Errors + Insider Misuse

  - Limiting Administrative / Elevated Rights (AD Audits)

  - Unique user ids (User and Service Accounts)

  - Role based access controls

Weighted (HIGH) – Regulatory data:

- HIPAA + PCI (Some of these items will be duplicated)

  - Encrypt sensitive ePHI in transmission – wireless

  - Encrypt data at rest

  - Two-Factor – credentialing and ID management

- Role based access / access controls in general (Need to know)

- AD / Limit elevated rights / Service Accounts

- Unique user IDs

- Password Management (Strength, Aging, Complexity)

- Automatic logoff / session timeouts

- Access logging (ePHI data)

- Isolate critical sensitive ePHI data / DLP

- Patch Management (OS and critical security patches)

- Outdated software and unsupported protocols (FTP, Telnet, etc.)

- Antivirus / endpoint management / malicious software detection

- Email (class all by itself) continues to be one of the most dangerous threat vectors that rises above all other vectors to the extent that it preys on unsuspecting, naive end users.

- Email remains one of the biggest threat vectors across the board. Email circumvents nearly all other security mitigation safeguards.

  - Training and Awareness

  - Anti-spoofing and smart email front-end anti-malware software

Security Prioritization - Conclusion

In conclusion, putting it all together, here is how I see health-care priorities in 2016 (for example):

1. **Two parallel tracks**

   1. **Ongoing Security Training / Education and Awareness**

   2. **Everything else**

Everything else: (Given- FWs, Proxies, IPS, Endpoint Management)

1. EMAIL (anti-spoofing, other tools) – Top of the list

2. Encryption (transmission-wireless / at rest / device) – Major Front-line defense

3. Two-Factor Authentication + Password management / strength / complexity / aging

4. Limit elevated and administrative rights + User account management (AD Controls)

5. Mobility and Device Management (smart phones, laptops)

6. Eliminate unsupported SW and insecure protocols (Outdated OS, FTP, Telnet, etc.)

7. Critical Patch Management (OS and critical patches within 1 quarter or less)

8. Endpoint Management Anti-Virus.

The methodology:

1. **Determine your annual and tactical sources (Verizon, Ponemon, and USCIRT).**
2. **Major security priority should be reviewed annually (Tactical Plan should be updated in Q4. prior to the New Year- exceptions are based on fiscal year and budgeting).**
3. **Security should be revisited Quarterly (looking for any macro changes in the threat landscape).**
4. **Strategic Plan should be reviewed semi-annually to adjust for any macro changes during the tactical year.**
5. **Note: Overall security priority (macro level) over the years has remained largely constant.**

NOTE: Remember that the parallel track is ongoing security education, training and awareness. Activities should constantly reflect progress in this area along with 'everything else'.

Security Strategy

Security strategy is a combination of both short-run tactical security and long-run strategy. The tactical security plan is really the operational focal point. Typically, tactical security looks 6 to 12 months out. Anything beyond 12 months in IT security, in my opinion, is strategic. The furthest I have successfully planned is probably 24 months. The landscape is constantly changing and evolving.

Tactical Security Plan

In the proceeding security section, I discussed these concepts.

Tactical security plans should be a direct outcome of the plan of action and milestones, which are a product of the Risk Assessment. There is a serial relationship. First you perform the appropriate Risk Assessment, then you develop the Plan of Action and Milestones, based on mid-level and high-level risks identified, and then you prioritize the plan of action using security prioritization concepts and create the tactical security plan.

Risk Assessment → Plan of Action & Milestones → Security Prioritization → Tactical Security Plan

29

Strategic Security Plan

The strategic security plan is really an attempt to look beyond the tactical focus. It considers implementations that could span year(s). Some risks take a long time to mitigate, particularly areas that require a lot of labor, reconfiguration work, and changes that impact all end users. These are the items that you roll into the strategic plan, in part, because of the length of time it will take to fully implement.

The other items require forward thinking and include trends and statistics. I am not big on guessing or taking chances for no good reason. So, I am going to say that 24 to 36 (on the high side) months is it.

→ Tactical Security Plan → Multi-year Goals & Objectives → Forward Looking → Strategic Plan

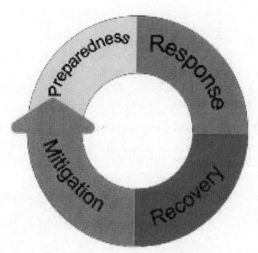

Incident Response Plan

The Incident Response Plan is one of the most important plans you can have.

Incident Handling process introduces four distinct phases:

preparation;

1. detection and analysis;
2. containment,
3. eradication and recovery; and

30

4. post-incident activity.

Each of these phases is iterative in nature.

There are many examples of Incident Response plans on the Internet. NIST is always the first place I look for templates, guides, and standards.

Here is a link at the time of this writing:

http://nvlpubs.nist.gov/nistpubs/SpecialPublications/NIST.SP.800-61r2.pdf

I cannot stress this enough, there is going to be an incident, and you will be graded on how well you handle it. Make sure you put the time into this plan, outlining all of the roles, and responsibilities.

It is a good idea to perform a mock Incident Response at least semi-annually.

Security Budget

Security budget is something that takes a lot of consideration. The budget needs to map to the Tactical and Strategic security plans.

My theory on IT security spending is negotiate. Nearly every product, hardware or software, is overpriced.

There is no reason you cannot reduce risks, increase security, and save money. I have saved businesses 100's of thousands of dollars over the years in capital purchases, while reducing the likelihood of a breach.

When it comes to product selection, the criteria should be function first and cohesion second. Let's face it, you cannot overlook the support side of the equation. However, all things being equal, if you can address the functional security requirement and save some money, why not?

Security Policy
The next few paragraphs are taken direct from the Sans.org site as I find them helpful.

Is it a Policy, a Standard or a Guideline?

What's in a name? We frequently hear people use the names "policy", "standard", and "guideline" to refer to documents that fall within the policy infrastructure. So that those who participate in this consensus process can communicate effectively, we'll use the following definitions.

A policy is typically a document that outlines specific requirements or rules that must be met. In the information/network security realm, policies are usually point-specific, covering a single area. For example, an **"Acceptable Use" policy** would cover the rules and regulations for appropriate use of the computing facilities.

A standard is typically a collection of system-specific or procedural-specific requirements that must be met by everyone. For example, you might have a standard that describes how to harden a Windows 8.1 workstation for placement on an external (DMZ) network. People must follow this standard exactly if they wish to install a Windows 8.1 workstation on an external network segment. In addition, a standard can be a technology selection, e.g. Company Name uses Tenable Security Center for continuous monitoring, and supporting policies and procedures define how it is used.

A guideline is typically a collection of system specific or procedural specific "suggestions" for best practice. They are not requirements to be met, but are strongly recommended. Effective security policies make frequent references to standards and guidelines that exist within an organization. Sans.org

Security Policies are part of the lifeblood of IT Security. They provide the underlying license to impose restrictions that nobody wants. Go team! There are a host of security policies that you need and here are just some of them (From Sans.org)

Network Security:

- Acquisition Assessment Policy
- Bluetooth Baseline Requirements Policy
- Remote Access Policy
- Remote Access Tools Policy
- Router and Switch Security Policy
- Wireless Communication Policy
- Wireless Communication Standard

Server Security:

- Database Credentials Policy
- Technology Equipment Disposal Policy
- Information Logging Standard
- Lab Security Policy
- Server Security Policy
- Software Installation Policy
- Workstation Security (For HIPAA) Policy

Application Security:

- Web Application Security Policy

Other Policies worth nothing is more general like Email, Internet Use, Acceptable Use.

However, there are two policies that are a 'MUST HAVE' Data Classification and Protection.

Data Classification & Protection

This section will focus on the critical need to classify data within an organization. One of the most challenging and daunting tasks for a security professional is to identify the critical and sensitive data within an organization. Yet for a security professional, it is one of the most fundamental and important things to do. Identifying critical assets (sensitive data) is necessary to apply security prioritization to critical servers housing it. You want to ensure that the fence you are building protects the sensitive data first, and everything else second.

The end-game here is two-fold. First, you need to properly classify all data within the organization -noting where the sensitive data resides. Sensitive data is defined as electronic Protected Health Information ('ePHI'), Payment Card Industry ('PCI'), and Personally Identifiable Information ('PII'). It is important to know exactly where the sensitive data resides, because everything done within the security context should be prioritized right down to which data to protect first. This is especially important when it comes to prioritizing security expenses.

Secondly, you want to develop a data protection standard. This is where you determine based on the sensitivity classification (risk) who should have access to it. It underlines the HIPAA concept of 'least privilege' and 'need to know.' Most organizations fail in this area with too many people having access to sensitive data.

Defining Data Classification

Data classification provides a way to ensure sensitive information is handled according to the risk it poses to the organization. All sensitive information should be labeled with a "risk level" that determines the methods and allowable resources for handling, the required encryption level, and storage and transmission requirements.

A good data loss prevention program depends on administrative controls and technical controls, such as data loss protection software. <u>By themselves, the technical controls are of little use unless an organization's employees understand how sensitive information should be handled</u>.

The following definitions were taken from the website:

**"http://searchsecurity.techtarget.com/feature/Tips-for-creating-a-data-classification-policy"
The article "Tips for creating a data classification policy", by Bill Hayes.**

Business Use Classification

The "business use only" classification label applies to information that is used in business processes, and [it is anticipated that] the unauthorized disclosure, modification or destruction of which is <u>not expected</u> to seriously affect the organization, customers, employees or business partners. Any information that is used in routine business matters -- such as internal policy manuals and company phone lists -- are good examples.

Confidential Classification

The confidential classification label applies to information that is used in sensitive business processes, [it is anticipated that] the unauthorized disclosure, modification or destruction of which will _adversely_ affect an organization, its customers, employees or business partners. Examples of sensitive information include intellectual property, contract negotiations, most personnel matters, _personally identifiable information (PII), protected health data (ePHI), bank account numbers and payment card information (PCI) of customers and employees._

Secret classification [highly confidential]

A data classification policy provides a way to ensure that sensitive information is handled according to the risk that it poses the organization, the types of sensitive information handled by the organization and compliance requirements.

Some organizations add an additional level, such as "secret" or "highly confidential" to label extremely sensitive information business processes, which the unauthorized disclosure, modification or destruction of would _seriously harm_ the organization, its customers, employees or business partners. Examples for health organizations include medical records relating to mental health, sexually transmitted diseases, HIV testing, and substance abuse. Examples for other organizations include documents used in mergers, strategic plans and litigation.

Making distinctions

Likewise, it may make sense for an organization to make a distinction between the sensitive information of customers and employees versus the sensitive information that applies only to company business processes. Classification labels, such as "personal confidential" and "business confidential" can be used in these instances.

Consideration: Rather than developing one overarching data classification policy, break up it up into several policies with associated procedures used to implement the policies.

Further guidance

The International Organization for Standardization (ISO) and the International Electro technical Commission (IEC) publication ISO/IEC 27002:2013 8.2.1 provides further guidance for handling sensitive information, as does NIST special publication NIST 800-60 volumes 1 and 2, _Guide for Mapping Types of Information and Information Systems to Security Categories._ Shon Harris discusses how to document data classification.

Tools to discover data

You should invoke the use of tools to find the sensitive data within an organization. Before you can begin the daunting task of classifying data, you must find it. For this you will need technology. It is far too time consuming to do manually, not to mention unreliable.

Enter Data Loss Prevention ('DLP'). This is the de'facto standard for data discovery. There are other components that make up DLP, which come into play during the enforcement of access and as part of data protection or Data Loss Prevention.

The discovery component of DLP is needed to find sensitive data housed on servers within an organization. To discover where the data resides you should perform an enterprise audit. Even with the proper technology this will take time, depending on the size of the organization and number of servers and/or storage devices in play.

Mechanisms for classifying data

To classify data, it is helpful to understand the applications that create, store, transmit, or process sensitive data. Therefore, it will be helpful to obtain a <u>complete list of applications</u> that involve sensitive data. This is a good first step.

The next step is to setup the DLP tool to <u>discover/scan the server infrastructure</u>. This can be prioritized based on known applications that involve sensitive data or generally subnet-by-subnet. Chances are you will likely want to scan all servers to validate any previous information provided. Interviews only go so far. Technology is required to accurately assess the nature of data stored within an organization. People and processes fail more often than technology.

The discovery process should be repeated based on the type of information you are looking for. It's all part of the classification process. There are no short cuts here. It takes time to do this right, but it's critical.

Classify the data discovered. The classifications provided in this paper are a good baseline, but may be changed to meet the specific data requirements of the business.

Data Classification Policy

The data classification policy should make clear the distinctions between data types. It should describe the proper handling of each.

Data Protection Policy

Data protection policy ensures the following:

- Complies with data classification policy and follows best practices and standards
- Protects data from unauthorized use and disclosure
- Protects the rights of staff, customers, and partners

The Role of Applications

The role of applications in terms of data classification and protection is clear. Applications provide access to the data. Therefore, access control mechanisms must be in place to ensure that access to sensitive data is properly authenticated, authorized and logged.

With the continued effort to share healthcare data and to improve overall patient care, protecting privacy has become a significant challenge.

The best way to ensure access is properly discriminated is by creating role based architecture. This way rights to access data are determined based on business 'need to know'.

Role based access

The concept of role based access makes perfect sense in the HealthCare industry. Clinicians need one level of access, healthcare providers need another, while administrators yet another.

However, if you think about it, role based access always makes sense in all industries.

A perfect complement to role based access is single sign-on. Organizations that can enhance the end-user experience while managing access control are a step ahead of most.

Data logging

Data logging is a function of auditing that is security and compliance based. HIPAA requires access to sensitive health data be logged. This is to ensure that there is no unauthorized access.

Traditional DLP tools include provisions for the following:

- Data Discovery

- Data Access Control/Audits
- Data Movement.

Putting it all together

So, let's put it all together. Data classification is an effort to audit data within the organization and classify it accordingly. The classification process should discriminate against sensitive and non-sensitive data. <u>Technology such as DLP is required to perform this audit</u>. An appropriate IS data classification policy must be established to properly assign classification to data found.

The data protection policy exists to ensure proper access controls are implemented to limit the access to data based on the concept of '<u>business need to know</u>'. The other components/modules that make up DLP beyond data discovery are necessary to further limit access to sensitive data (based on your role) and log appropriate access accordingly.

This effort is largely one-part data discovery, one-part data classification, and one huge part data protection. The natural extrapolation of the protection part includes, classifying servers as sensitive or not, applying the appropriate security controls to ensure the servers/data are adequately protected -and in the final analysis available and secure.

Data Classification & Protection - Conclusion

In conclusion, you will need to prioritize this effort. It is critical to understand where the sensitive data is within the organization. Discovery and classification go together. Protecting the critical and sensitive data is the primary function of information security.

Once the sensitive data within the organization is identified, then the security prioritization strategy can be applied to it. We want to affirm the business of healthcare by finding ways to enhance the end-user and patient care experience, while keeping sensitive data secure and protecting patient's privacy rights.

Security Training and Awareness

Security Training and Awareness is something you can never have too much of. As I have outlined under security prioritization, it is a constant and parallel track to 'everything else' that is security.

There needs to be several core areas in place and you should plan to address each of the following:

1. New Hire Training.
2. Routine Monthly/Quarterly mini training sessions to encompass the major threats of the day such as Spear Phishing. Typically, a Learning Management System (LMS) would suffice for this.
3. Seminars or Lunch and Learn sessions that reach out to every major department from HR, to Finance, Marketing, and more.
4. Email distribution list(s) for Alerts and Breaking News that impact staff.
5. Newsletter or Security Web Page to inform staff of initiatives and changes everyone needs to know about.

Quarterly Security Reviews

Quarterly reviews are the operational equivalent to ongoing checkups. They are designed to address vulnerability status, progress toward mitigating risks, performance against the tactical security plan, and are critical to ongoing security operations.

Here are some of the things that you will want to review or perform during a Quarterly Security Review:

1. Review Access Control (New Hires, Terms, and Changes).
2. Review the impact of security changes made during the quarter.
3. Run Vulnerability scans internal.
4. Perform external penetration tests.
5. General Policy Review.
6. General Procedure Review.
7. Review major security initiatives and progress toward Tactical Plan.
8. Creation of a Quarterly Security Report for executive management and senior leadership.

Normally, I dedicate an entire week to running the tests, reviewing everything, and creating the report for executive management.

Annual Refresh

The Annual refresh consists of several major tasks that must be completed. Performing an annual refresh can take weeks, and I usually allow an entire month.

Here are some of the things that must be completed:

1. Annual Risk Assessment (NIST/HIPAA/PCI DSS).
2. Updated Plan of Action and Milestones.
3. Updated / New Tactical Security Plan for the coming year.

Assuming you are on a Calendar year basis, I would normally perform an Annual refresh during December. It's usually a slow month, lots of vacations, and you can focus. However, let me make a key point on the selection. You want to tie in with the budget planning as most of the time tactical plans include purchases. If not the current year, perhaps the next, so make sure it coincides with budget planning.

Security Organizational Models

There are multiple security models that are consistent with today's practices.

Single person operation

A single person operation usually exists once an organization begins to realize the critical need for security. Typically, they will start with an Information Security Manager. This person is the best candidate for this guide. This guide is designed to provide detail about all of the various critical functions needed to build a security program from scratch.

In the case of a single person operation, you will need to put together a road-map of things to get done. You will need to focus on the following key building blocks, and quickly:

- Performing a Risk Assessment (NIST/HIPAA/PCI DSS)
- Developing a Plan of Action and Milestones
- Tactical Security Plan
- Policy Development
- Security Awareness and Training
- Quarterly Reviews
- Annual Refresh

These building blocks will be critical and the top three items need to be done within the first 90 days (depending on the size of the organization 30-60 days). The 90-day track is on the high side and more typical of a large, complex organization. I would say overall 60 days is a good average. If you can produce the top 3 items within the first 60 days, you will be well on your way to developing a solid security program.

Since you will not have a team to delegate security efforts too, you will need to spend a fair amount of time developing relationships with your peers and other members of the IT department.

You need to focus on network engineering, desktop support, systems administration, and applications. All these areas are critical to security, and you will need their support to get things done. You will need support from HR, Payroll, Accounting and many other departments over time, but the aforementioned will make or break your operation and any plans of success you have for the security program.

No other model requires you to be more effective for the simple reason, you are going to need to borrow from your peers staff to accomplish many, perhaps most, of your security tactical activities.

Small Team

The small team structure normally includes an Information Security Manager and 1 to 2 people.

Typically, that would mean a security engineer and a security analyst. The kind of duties that each one would have is loosely as follows:

Security Engineer:

- Security Design and Implementation
- Hands-on deployment of the following:
    - Firewalls
    - Proxies
    - IPS/IDS
    - Network Threat Protection Appliances
    - Advanced Malware Protection Appliances
    - Security Appliances in general

Security Analyst:

- Operational Review and Analysis
- Security Event Incident Management
- Access Control

- Forensics
- Anti-Virus / Anti-Malware

The general distinction is that the security engineer is largely involved in security design decisions and the initial configuration and deployment and to some degree ongoing hands-on maintenance and support of security appliances, HW and SW.

The security analyst is more concerned with the operations of the security appliances, log analysis, forensics, and general configuration. They are involved with a lot of the day to day activities and upkeep.

A three-man team with a manager with a solid background in hands-on network and security engineering can go a long way toward managing a medium to large organization.

Large Team

The Large team model is just an extension of the small team model where additional functions are segregated and more specialized. The total security team, if you will, looks a lot like this with the following skillsets:

- Sr. Security Engineer
  - Security Design, Primary Lead for team, the 'go to' person in security
  - Equipment purchase, configuration and initial deployment
  - Oversight, coaching and mentoring the team
  - Troubleshooting
- Security Engineer
  - Security design, but subordinate to the senior security design engineer
  - Testing, configuration, and deployment
  - Security Event and Incident Management (SEIM)
  - Forensics
- Security Operations Engineer
  - Operations, Day to Day security activities
  - Configuration, ongoing maintenance
  - Anti-virus and Anti-malware
  - Desktop support and laptop/mobile device support
  - Email, Spam and malicious attachments
- Security Analyst(s)
  - Log Analysis
  - Forensics Analysis
  - General security support
  - Reporting

- Security Identity and Access Management (IAM)
  - Access Control
  - Active Directory / Windows OS
  - Analysis and Reporting.

When Organizational Changes are needed

In many cases networking/technology and security are separate. By separate, they report to different managers. Over the years I have seen two scenarios, common manager and disparate manager.

One of the primary drivers for organizational change is in fact an attempt to realign networking and security under a common manager. The issue of separating them is tied to checks and balances. I get that. I maintain, let Internal Audit be the cop.

However, in the end, you have to work together, there has to be tight cohesion between networking and security. And most of the drivers for organizational change are tied to resolving dysfunction, lack of cohesion, turf wars, personalities, and so forth.

I conclude, that if you have the option, it is better to have both network and security engineers report to the same manager. It is just easier and way more efficient.

Disparate Manager

There are two ways to address this problem. Either reorganize under a single manager or establish a collaborative team with joint network and security members. It is much easier to create a collaborative team made up of individuals from networking and security than it is to align everyone under a single manager. The reason being is that you already have two managers and both sets of managers probably already have alliances. Also, HR has to get involved.

Common Manager

The best way to do this is out of the gate. It is easier than trying to retrofit later. If you choose to do this once the teams split, you will have to campaign, work with everyone on both sides, HR, and convince your manager it is the only way.

So, here is the thing. If you are building and augmenting, keep network and security under the same manager. If you have already split off, use collaborative teams (at least in the short run).

Operational Effectiveness

I want to talk about organizational effectiveness. It is the sum product of many of the components that I have laid out. To achieve progress operationally you should have a plan, you need support of peers and many others (the CIO), you need to communicate effectively within and without IT, you need to prioritize your efforts, and you need to report on progress.

I am a strong believer in the concept of a Project Management Organization (PMO) to help drive long-term IT security initiatives. I think having a PMO arm inside of IT is a great thing when used appropriately with the right personnel. It can also cause delays. The PMO should never be in a position where it is playing catch up against network or security operational activities.

Take the time to convert your tactical security plan into an overall project plan with timelines, monthly objectives, and where possible incentives for the team. Let's face it people are always your number one asset.

Communications and Executive Buy-in

The concept of communications and executive buy-in is not new. For any security program to succeed YOU must have executive buy-in at least at the CIO level. CIO buy-in is a must to succeed in building, sustaining, or augmenting a security program. I want to stress this point; it is the number one building block without which success will be elusive -guaranteed.

In the 'good book', stressing a word three times means make no mistake this is important. CIO Buy-in, CIO Buy-in, CIO Buy-in. Let's see what happens. If you only take away this concept from the entire document, it will have been worth the purchase.

Until the CSO reports directly to the CEO, and I can make a strong case for it, it is not really your job to convince the CEO. There are other C-level executives that could function as allies, but practically speaking, you just need the CIO to be on board.

Communication is fundamental in IT. There is never enough of it. Communication needs to happen bi-directionally between you and the CIO. It needs to happen amongst your peers, and very effectively outside IT to the entire end user population.

Lack of communication is the number one beef I constantly hear. Develop avenues of communication that meet the above targeted audiences. There needs to be mechanisms to communicate and gain support bi-directionally from the CIO, peer meetings and communication strategies, and a very effective communication vehicle for the outside IT, end-user community. Adjust your communication in writing to align with your audience. As an executive coach, I have spent a tremendous amount of time conveying the concept that words are powerful; use them wisely to accomplish your objectives.

Writing that Works

In my experience, there are three levels of writing. The first level is the average writer that has a basic command of the English language. In IT, these folks can write, but everything comes out technical, and in nearly no-way do they convey IT topics effectively to non-IT personnel. The second level is an effective communicator that usually gains acceptance based on their writing skills alone. And the third level are the very few that are masterful in their writing to the point of winning over their staunchest criticizers.

The better writer the better the outcome.

Executive Reporting

The second most valuable thing you can do in IT security in terms of reporting is to report progress to executives like the CIO on a routine basis. Obviously real progress toward reducing risk and better protecting sensitive information is the goal, but reporting is a close second.

Security is a pro-active strategy, the idea is to not bring up failings, breaches, losses in any fashion. So, reporting is important, because it's an opportunity to justify why you invested in various products in the first place. The reason you have not had a recent malware outbreak is in part, because you invested in the following tools to reduce the likelihood.

It is the CIO, in today's organizational structure, that must acquire the funding for IT security purchases. So, arm him with lots of quantitative data that underlines progress toward ultimate security within your organization. Produce a report monthly that captures your overall progress toward tactical and strategic plans.

There are not many canned reports on the Internet that really do this area of reporting justice. I have looked around. So, I am going to provide a sample that I think is useful. What makes IT security reporting so challenging is the question of what to report on.

How to communicate security performance to executives

The best way to do this is a report that captures progress in one to two pages. Simple but effective. The goal is to report progress on various elements of the security program. Many times, the values are quantitative, but many are not. I have included a sample report / dashboard that captures a lot of different areas that collectively are part of the total IT security solution.

Sample Reports

Below is a sample report that I have used to demonstrate progress on nearly everything that I could think of on one page. Granted it is busy. There are many ways to report on progress, and many tools provide reports, the trick is at a glance providing data that is clear and demonstrates the value proposition associated with IT security spending.

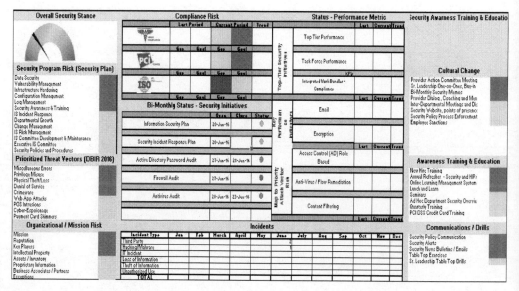

Putting it all together

So, from the standpoint of building an IT security program, there are many building blocks and I have tried to talk at some level about each of them. Here they are again at a high level:

- Risk Assessments (Identifying the State of Security within your Organization)
- Plan of Action and Milestones
- Security Prioritization
- Tactical and Strategic Planning
- Operational Effectiveness
- Security Policy Development
- Budgeting
- Training and Awareness
- Executive Reporting

Conclusion

In this guide, I have tried to touch on all the aspects of building a security program. Clearly, I could have spent pages and pages talking about each element, but my goal was to provide a footprint, a blueprint, a roadmap if you will to get started. To provide insight on areas that are critical, and to help you avoid roadblocks.

I have spent more time in some sections, because they are concepts that I think deserve a great deal of focus. One of the overarching beliefs that I have is that everything that is security has a priority. This is important, because in my estimation, there are never enough security resources to go around, and you want to be highly efficient in terms of where you apply energy and resources in a way that always reduces the maximum number of risks. And you want to be always mindful of ways to improve security while spending less money. IT security professionals need to negotiate often.

The person responsible for security must have a complete vision of where they want to take the security program, and will need a roadmap to get there. Therefore, I wrote this guide.

So, in conclusion here are the critical elements that I believe are needed by the CSO to build a successful security program:

- Strong leadership skills with expertise within both contexts of the 80/20 rule
- IT security credentials such as the CISSP
- Strategy for performing Risk Assessments & Plan of Action and Milestones
- Abundance of knowledge about regulatory requirements
- Strong planning skills both tactical and strategic
- Strong interpersonal skills that can draw people together even with opposing views
- Solid communications, both written and verbal
- Support from the CIO
- Peer support
- A mentor and a coach.

I hope that this guide helps you navigate through the task of improving security at your organization. Nearly every organization could improve its security and you can make a difference. I hope this helps you out.

References and bibliography

ALE, acronyms.com, https://en.wikipedia.org/wiki/Annualized_loss_expectancy

CISSP, HCISPP, www.isc2.org

HIPAA, http://www.hhs.gov

International Organization for Standardization (ISO), www.iso.org

Mindful Resources, http://mindfulsecurity.com/2009/02/03/policies-standards-and-guidelines/

NIST, http://csrc.nist.gov/

Ponemon, www.ponemon.org

PCI DSS, www.pcisecuritystandards.org

SANs, www.sans.org

Searchsecurity.techtarget.com, www.searchsecurity.techtarget.com/feature/Tips-for-creating-a-data-classification-policy

USCirt, www.us-cert.gov

Verizon DBIR 2015, Verizon, www.verizonenterprise.com/DBIR/2015

Made in the USA
Lexington, KY
15 June 2017